Hamlet

WILLIAM SHAKESPEARE

Level 3

Retold by Chris Rice
Series Editors: Andy Hopkins and Jocelyn Potter

Pearson Education Limited
Edinburgh Gate, Harlow,
Essex CM20 2JE, England
and Associated Companies throughout the world.

ISBN-10: 1-4058-3101-4
ISBN-13: 978-1-4058-3101-7

This edition first published by Penguin Books 2006

Typeset by Graphicraft Limited, Hong Kong
Set in 11/14pt Bembo
Printed in China
SWTC/01

Produced for the Publishers by
Graphicraft Productions Limited, Dartford, UK

Published by Pearson Education Limited in association with
Penguin Books Ltd, both companies being subsidiaries of Pearson Plc

For a complete list of the titles available in the Penguin Readers series please write to your local
Pearson Education office or to: Penguin Readers Marketing Department, Pearson Education,
Edinburgh Gate, Harlow, Essex, CM20 2JE

Contents

Introduction

'Oh, how can a great man fall so low? A prince, a student, a soldier, the flower of his country, the mirror of everyone's dreams – all gone! He was so brave, clever and beautiful. He was the most perfect of men. He filled my ears with the sweet music of his promises. But now he fills them with the crazy words of a broken mind.'

Ophelia is in love with Hamlet, the Prince of Denmark, but Hamlet is acting very strangely. Why is he so rude to her? Why is his heart filled with so much sadness and angry pain? Is he really mad, or does he have a secret plan?

Only two people know Hamlet's real secret – his good friends Marcellus and Horatio – but they have promised not to tell anyone. Hamlet wants revenge! His wicked uncle, Claudius, has murdered his father and married his mother, and Hamlet wants to punish him. But how? Will the young prince be strong and brave enough to take his revenge? Will he succeed in destroying the wickedness that is destroying him?

Hamlet is one of the most famous plays in the world, and it is as true and alive today as it was four hundred years ago. In a world of lies and murder, Hamlet is different. He is honest and thoughtful. He believes in goodness. But he is not perfect. He is an ordinary man who makes mistakes. Often, he cannot decide what to do. This is what makes him, and the play, so special. There are no simple answers to difficult questions. There is no easy promise of happiness for good people in a bad world.

This is a story full of death – murder, accidents, illness and graves. But there *is* a message of hope. It *is* possible for even the weakest of people to be brave. And we can learn something good about ourselves when we are suffering the most terrible pain.

Hamlet decides to fight the wickedness of the world and the shadows in his heart at the same time. Perhaps he will succeed – and perhaps not. But it is important that he has tried. He will become a better person.

Hamlet was Shakespeare's 25th play, and it was written between 1598 and 1602. It is the story of a young Danish prince who lived 1,700 years ago. The story of Hamlet is found in early European literature: the first example was in 1250. A play with the same story was produced a short time before 1589, and it was very popular in London theatres between 1594 and 1596. Shakespeare made the story into the beautifully-written play that we all know today. It is still acted in theatres all around the world. People are always discovering something new and interesting about it.

There have also been many films of *Hamlet*. One of the most successful was made in 1996, with Kenneth Branagh as Hamlet, Julie Christie as Gertrude and Kate Winslet as Ophelia. Many world-famous actors are in it, even in the smallest parts. For example, Robin Williams is Osric and Gerard Depardieu is only a messenger! The film is four hours' long, but it was a great success at the cinema.

William Shakespeare (1564–1616) is the most famous writer of plays in the English language. He was born in Stratford-upon-Avon, in England. He went to a good school, but did not go to university. In 1582, he married Anne Hathaway and had three children. By 1592, he was famous in London as an actor and writer. Over the next twenty years he wrote thirty-seven plays and many famous poems. He sometimes wrote three plays a year! His plays were very popular, and many of them were acted in front of King James I.

Reading and acting the play

You can read *Hamlet* silently, like every other story in a book. You will have to imagine the places, the people's clothes and their voices from the words on the page.

But Shakespeare did not write *Hamlet* as literature for reading. He wrote it for actors on a theatre stage. You can read the play in a group with other people. This is very different from silent reading. You can speak the words and bring the people in the play to life. They can sound happy or sad, worried or angry. You can add silences and important noises, like the sound of music or guns. You can also stop and discuss the play. What does this person mean? Why does he/she say that?

But you can have more fun if you act the play. *Hamlet* has a lot of exciting scenes. There are also some beautiful speeches. The people in the play have to show a lot of different feelings. If you act the play, you can show these feelings by your words *and* actions.

Most of the story happens inside a large castle. You should think about the furniture in the rooms – nice tables and chairs, beautiful curtains, pictures on the walls. You should also think about the clothes – a lot of gold and silver for the King and Queen, soldier's clothes for the Ghost, simpler clothes for Hamlet and Ophelia. You will need some special equipment, too, like swords. In some scenes, there are only two or three people talking, but in others there are crowds. You will have to think about where people sit or stand in the large rooms at court. And you will also have to plan the big swordfight at the end.

Hamlet is a wonderful play. You can read it or act it. But have fun and enjoy it!

The People in the Play

HAMLET, Prince of Denmark
CLAUDIUS, King of Denmark, Hamlet's uncle
GERTRUDE, Queen of Denmark, Hamlet's mother
POLONIUS, the most important man at the King's court
OPHELIA, Polonius's daughter
LAERTES, Polonius's son
THE GHOST of Hamlet's father

HORATIO, Hamlet's friend
ROSENCRANTZ, Hamlet's old schoolfriend
GUILDENSTERN, Hamlet's old schoolfriend
MARCELLUS, a soldier, Hamlet's friend

OSRIC, a lord at the King's court
VOLTEMAND, the King's messenger to Norway
CORNELIUS, the King's messenger to Norway
FORTINBRAS, Prince of Norway

FIRST ACTOR
SECOND ACTOR
THIRD ACTOR

BARNARDO, a soldier
A WORKMAN
A SAILOR
A MESSENGER at the King's court
A MESSENGER from England
A CHURCHMAN

OTHER LORDS and LADIES at the King's court
SERVANTS at the King's court
SOLDIERS and OFFICERS at the King's court
SOLDIERS with Fortinbras

Act 1   The Ghost on the Castle Wall

Scene 1   The largest room in the King's castle

[*There is a platform at one end of the room, with beautiful chairs for the King and Queen. Polonius, Laertes, Hamlet, Ophelia, Voltemand, Cornelius and other lords and ladies are waiting around the platform. Music plays. Claudius and Gertrude come in and stand on the platform in front of their chairs.*]

CLAUDIUS [*to everybody*]: The memory of our king, my dear brother, is still fresh in all our hearts. The sadness of his death will be with us for ever, but we must begin to think of other things. So, with one eye wet and the other eye dry, I have taken my brother's sister, the Queen, as my wife. We married with your permission, and for this we thank you. But some people think that our grief has made us weak. Young Fortinbras of Norway is planning to attack our country. He wants to take back from us his father's lost land. This is land that my brother won honestly and bravely many years ago. [*holding up a letter*] I have written to young Fortinbras's uncle, the King of Norway. The old King is weak, and cannot leave his bed. He knows nothing about his nephew's unlawful plans for war against us. [*to Cornelius and Voltemand*] Take this letter to the King as quickly as you can. We do not have much time. [*Voltemand and Cornelius take the letter and leave. Claudius turns to Laertes with a warm smile.*] And now, Laertes, you have something to ask me? No man at this court is more important to me than your father, so do not be shy. Tell me what you want.

LAERTES: My Lord, I came back to Denmark to see you become king. Now I would like to return to France.

CLAUDIUS [*to Polonius*]: Does he have your permission?

1

POLONIUS: With a heavy heart, I agree.

CLAUDIUS [*to Laertes*]: You have my permission, too. [*turning to Hamlet*] But now, my nephew Hamlet, and my son . . .

HAMLET [*angrily to himself*]: I am more than a nephew, but less than a son!

CLAUDIUS: Why are you still so unhappy?

HAMLET [*with a cold smile*]: How can I be unhappy, my Lord, when you are so kind to me?

GERTRUDE [*softly*]: Dear Hamlet, stop wearing those black clothes and be friendly to our new king. You must stop feeling sad about your father. We all have to die one day.

HAMLET [*coldly*]: Yes, Madam, we do. But my grief is more than just black clothes, sad speeches and eyes full of tears. My grief is *real*. It is inside me. You cannot see the true sadness in my heart.

CLAUDIUS: All men lose their fathers, and a son must feel sadness. But too much sadness is not the grief of a real man. It is a crime against God, against the dead, even a crime against reason. So throw away this useless grief and think of me as your father. After me, you will be the next king. And my love for you is as great as the love of a father for his son. I know that you want to return to your studies in Wittenberg. But I want you to stay here with me. Then I can see you every day. You are the most important person at my court.

GERTRUDE: Stay here with us, Hamlet. Don't go to Wittenberg.

HAMLET [*to Gertrude*]: I will do what you ask, Madam.

CLAUDIUS [*smiling at Gertrude*]: Come, Madam. Hamlet's sensible words have pleased my heart. Let's open the wine and drink to our happiness and to the health of Denmark!

[*Music plays. Everybody leaves except Hamlet.*]

HAMLET [*angrily and unhappily*]: Why is it against God's law for a man to kill himself? Oh God, the world seems a tired, empty, useless place to me! How can things go so wrong so quickly? My father's only been dead for two months. He was a wonderful king, and so loving to my mother. He was everything to her. But less than a month after his death – oh, I can't even think of it! Weakness, your name is Woman! Less than a month after his death, this grief-filled woman married my uncle! Less than a month – before the salt of her dishonest tears turned her eyes red! Oh, what a wicked woman, to hurry so quickly to the bed of her dead husband's brother! My heart is breaking, [*noticing the arrival of Horatio, Marcellus and Barnardo*] but it must break quietly. I must say nothing more.

HORATIO: Greetings, my Lord.

HAMLET [*smiling*]: Horatio! What are you doing in Elsinore? I thought you were in Wittenberg.

HORATIO: My Lord, I came when I heard about your father's death.

HAMLET [*quietly*]: Yes, that was the worst day of my life.

HORATIO: I saw your father once. He was a good king.

HAMLET: He was a man. There won't be a man like him again.

HORATIO [*nervously*]: My Lord, I think I saw him last night.

HAMLET [*surprised*]: Saw? Who?

HORATIO: The King, your father. Three nights ago, these two good men, Marcellus and Barnardo, saw your father's ghost while they were on guard on the castle wall. They saw him again the next night. Dressed like a soldier, he walked past them slowly. He then disappeared into the shadows as they watched. Last night, I joined them on guard and I saw him too. It was exactly as they described it. It *was* your father.

HAMLET: Did you speak to him?

HORATIO: We did, my Lord, but he didn't reply.

HAMLET: Did he look angry?

HORATIO: More sad than angry.

HAMLET: What colour was his beard?

HORATIO: The same as when he was alive – black mixed with silver.

HAMLET [*excitedly*]: I'll join you on guard tonight. Perhaps he'll come again. If it *is* my father, I'll speak to him. But please, don't tell *anyone* about this. It must be our secret. I'll meet you on the castle wall just before midnight. Until then, goodbye. [*Horatio, Marcellus and Barnardo leave.*] My father's ghost! Dressed like a soldier! All is not well. No good will come of this. Something bad's going to happen – and nothing in the world will stop it. [*He leaves.*]

Scene 2   *Ophelia's room in the castle*

[*In the room are a bed, a chair and a table with a mirror on it. Ophelia is sitting at the mirror, tidying her hair. Polonius comes in.*]

POLONIUS [*angrily*]: I've heard that you and Hamlet are spending a lot of time together. If it's true, I'm not happy. Be honest with me. What's happening between you and Hamlet?

OPHELIA [*softly*]: He's shown many signs of love for me.

POLONIUS [*pulling Ophelia to her feet and shaking her roughly by the arms*]: Signs of love? You speak like a child. You're too young to understand the real meaning of these things. Do you believe these 'signs', as you call them?

OPHELIA [*shaking her head and crying*]: I don't know, my Lord.

POLONIUS: These 'signs' of love are not the real thing. You must be more careful, or you'll get into trouble.

OPHELIA: My Lord, he's always acted well towards me. When he speaks of love, he seems to mean it.

POLONIUS: I'm sure he does. When a young man's blood burns with love, his tongue easily finds fine words. But believe me, these words have no meaning. I order you to stay away from him. [*turning away and pulling her by the arm*] Now, come with me.

4

OPHELIA [*unhappily*]: All right, my Lord.

[*They leave.*]

Scene 3   The castle wall at night

[*There is a full moon and the ground is covered with snow. Hamlet, Horatio and Marcellus arrive.*]

HAMLET: It's cold out here. What time is it?
MARCELLUS: Twelve o'clock.

[*The Ghost arrives.*]

HORATIO [*excitedly*]: Look, my Lord, it's here.
HAMLET [*seeing the Ghost*]: God help us! Are you from Heaven or from Hell? King, Father, speak to me! Why has your dead body left your grave? Why do you walk around in the moonlight in soldiers' clothes?

[*The Ghost makes a sign with his finger for Hamlet to follow.*]

HORATIO: It's calling you. It has a secret to tell you.
MARCELLUS: It wants you to follow it. But don't go.
HAMLET: If it refuses to speak to me here, I must follow it.
HORATIO [*nervously*]: No, my Lord!
HAMLET [*calmly*]: Why not? I'm not afraid of it.
MARCELLUS [*holding Hamlet's arm*]: You mustn't go!
HAMLET [*angrily*]: Take your hands off me! I'll make a ghost of anyone who tries to stop me!

[*Marcellus takes his hands away. The Ghost leaves and Hamlet follows.*]

HORATIO: He's listening too much to his imagination.
MARCELLUS: We must follow him. We have to protect him.

[*They leave.*]

Scene 4   *A dark, snowy forest*

[*Hamlet arrives, following the Ghost.*]

HAMLET [*stopping*]: Where are you taking me? Speak, or I refuse to walk another step.

GHOST [*stopping and turning round*]: I am the ghost of your father. I have to spend my nights in darkness and my days in the fires of Hell until someone has paid for the crime against me. Listen to me, and listen to me well. If you love your father, you must punish his murderer.

HAMLET [*crying*]: Oh, God! Murder?

GHOST: Yes, the worst kind of murder. It was reported that I was killed by a wild animal in the garden. But that is a lie. My murderer was the animal who is now the king.

HAMLET: I knew it! My uncle?

GHOST: Yes. With his clever words and wicked mind, he won the heart of my queen. I loved her with an honest heart, but now she has accepted the love of a dog! She is a weak woman. But morning is near – I must hurry with my story. One afternoon, I was sleeping in my garden as usual. While I was asleep, your uncle poured poison into my ears. In this way, I was robbed of my life, my country and my queen. If you love your father, you must punish his wicked brother for his crime. But do not lift an angry hand against your mother. Leave her for God to judge. Now it is almost morning and I must hurry away. Goodbye, my son, goodbye. Remember me. [*He leaves.*]

HAMLET [*holding his head and crying*]: Oh, Heaven, Earth – yes, even Hell – what new suffering can you throw at me? But I must be strong. Remember you? Oh yes, dear Father. None of my other memories are important to me now. I will not rest until I have revenge!

'Oh, God! Murder?'

[*Horatio and Marcellus arrive.*]

HORATIO [*worried*]: Heaven protect him! What news, my Lord?

HAMLET [*smiling strangely*]: Oh, wonderful!

HORATIO: That's good, my Lord. Tell us.

HAMLET: No, because you'll tell others about it.

HORATIO [*surprised and hurt*]: We won't, my Lord!

HAMLET [*wildly*]: No one will ever believe what the ghost has just told me. There's no one more wicked in all Denmark. But let's go our different ways – you to your business, I to mine.

HORATIO: These are wild words, my Lord.

HAMLET: I'm sorry if you feel bad.

HORATIO: There's no reason for us to feel bad, my Lord.

HAMLET: Oh, there is, Horatio! But, good friends, will you do one last thing for me? Tell no one what you've seen tonight.

HORATIO and MARCELLUS: We promise.

HAMLET [*taking out his sword*]: Promise on my sword.

HORATIO [*coldly*]: We've already promised, my Lord.

GHOST'S VOICE [*from below the stage*]: Promise on his sword!

HAMLET [*laughing*]: Ha, ha. Did you hear that voice from under the ground?

HORATIO [*frightened*]: Oh, this is very strange.

HAMLET: There are more things in Heaven and Earth than you've ever dreamt of, Horatio. After this, you'll think *I'm* strange too, even crazy. But it will be an act – it won't be real. You'll know my secret, but you mustn't tell. Now promise.

MARCELLUS and HORATIO [*putting their hands on Hamlet's sword*]: We promise.

HAMLET: So, dear friends, let's go back to the castle together. Remember, not a word to anyone. These are strange times. But the unhappiest time of all was the day that I was born.

[*They leave.*]

Act 2   The Mad Prince

Scene 1   *Polonius's room in the castle*

[*In the room are a bed, a desk with books, pens and paper on it, and a simple wooden chair. Polonius is sitting at the desk. Ophelia comes in, looking frightened.*]

POLONIUS [*standing up, worried*]: Ophelia, what's the matter?

OPHELIA: Oh, my Lord, I'm so frightened. While I was sitting in my room, Lord Hamlet came in with a crazy look in his eyes.

POLONIUS: What did he say to you?

OPHELIA: He took me by the wrist and looked at me strangely for a long time. Then, without a word, he walked out of the room, looking at me over his shoulder.

POLONIUS: This seems to be the madness of love. Have you been unkind to him since I last saw you?

OPHELIA: I only did what you told me. I sent back all his letters and refused to see him.

POLONIUS: I'm sorry, Ophelia. Perhaps I was wrong about him. I was afraid that he was just playing with you. I didn't want him to hurt you. We must tell the King about this immediately.

[*They leave.*]

Scene 2   *A large room in the castle*

[*In the room are a large fireplace, a long table and many comfortable chairs. Pictures, swords and mirrors are hanging on the walls. There are two doors: the main double doors, and a small door at the back of the room. Claudius and Gertrude are standing in the middle of the room. Their servants are waiting behind them. Rosencrantz and Guildenstern come in through the main doors.*]

CLAUDIUS: Welcome, dear Rosencrantz and Guildenstern. It is always good to see you. But I called you here for an urgent reason. You have heard about the change in Prince Hamlet? He is acting very strangely. I cannot understand the reason for it, but perhaps it is still sadness at his father's death. You are two of his oldest friends. Spend some time with him. He will feel comfortable in your company. If you can discover the reasons for his strangeness, it will help us all.

GERTRUDE: There is nobody that my son likes more than you. If you can help us, we shall both be very grateful.

GUILDENSTERN: We are proud to help.

GERTRUDE: Could you visit my poor son immediately? [*to two of the servants*] Take these two men to Hamlet.

[*Rosencrantz and Guildenstern leave with the servants. Voltemand and Cornelius come in with Polonius.*]

CLAUDIUS: Welcome, my dear friends. What news from Norway?

VOLTEMAND: The old King was very sad and angry when he read your letter. He told his nephew to stop his plans for war against us immediately. Fortinbras agreed, and this pleased the King. So he gave his nephew permission to take his soldiers into Poland. [*giving Claudius a letter*] He requests permission for Fortinbras and his soldiers to pass quietly through our country.

CLAUDIUS [*looking quickly at the letter*]: This is good news, but I will think about it later. Thank you for your excellent work. Go and rest. Tonight we shall eat together and have a party!

[*Voltemand and Cornelius go out, leaving the main doors open.*]

POLONIUS: I have more good news for you, my Lord and Lady. I have discovered why Prince Hamlet is acting strangely. He is mad with love for my daughter. [*holding up a letter*] She has given me this. Listen, and you will understand. [*reading*] *To beautiful Ophelia, I have little skill with words. I do not have the language to describe my pain. But I love you. I am yours for ever, my*

10

dear Lady, for long as this body is mine. Hamlet. [*looking up from the letter*] My daughter showed me this letter immediately, and all the others that he has sent.

CLAUDIUS: How has she received these words of love?

POLONIUS: I told her to lock herself in her room and to receive no messengers or gifts. She wisely followed my orders. As a result, the Prince fell into sadness. He stopped eating and sleeping. In the end, he became the madman that we all pity today.

CLAUDIUS [*to Gertrude*]: Do you think this is true?

GERTRUDE [*sadly*]: It seems possible.

POLONIUS: I will prove that I am right.

CLAUDIUS: How?

POLONIUS: You know that he likes to walk alone around this castle – sometimes for many hours?

GERTRUDE: Yes, I have noticed.

POLONIUS: I will send my daughter to him during one of these walks. We can hide in the shadows and watch them. If I am wrong about his love for my daughter, I will become a farmer.

CLAUDIUS: All right. Let's see what happens.

[*Hamlet comes in through the open main doors, reading a book.*]

GERTRUDE [*quietly*]: Look. There's the poor boy.

POLONIUS: Forgive me, my Lord and Lady, but you must go quickly. Leave me to speak to him alone. [*Claudius and Gertrude leave through the small door at the back of the room.*] How are you, my Lord Hamlet?

HAMLET: Well, thank God.

POLONIUS: Do you know who I am?

HAMLET: I know you very well. You're a fish-seller.

POLONIUS: No, I'm not.

HAMLET: That's a pity, because fish-sellers are very honest men. Have you got a daughter?

POLONIUS: I have, my Lord.

HAMLET: She must stay out of the sun. It's dangerous for her health.

POLONIUS [*quietly to himself*]: He's completely mad. But when I was young, I also suffered for love. I was almost as mad as he is now. I'll speak to him again. [*to Hamlet*] What are you reading, my Lord?

HAMLET: Words, words, words.

POLONIUS: What are they about?

HAMLET: Lies. The writer says here that old men have grey beards, small minds and weak legs. It is, of course, all true. But it's wrong to write about it.

POLONIUS [*quietly to himself*]: He's mad, but he's not stupid. I'll leave him now, and send my daughter to him. [*to Hamlet*] My Lord, I must go now. Goodbye. [*He leaves through the main doors.*]

HAMLET [*quietly to himself*]: Stupid old man!

[*Guildenstern and Rosencrantz come in.*]

GUILDENSTERN and ROSENCRANTZ: My dearest Lord!

HAMLET [*smiling*]: My dear friends, how are you both? What brings you to Elsinore?

ROSENCRANTZ: We came to visit you, my Lord.

HAMLET: Was this your idea, or did someone ask you to come?

GUILDENSTERN [*laughing nervously*]: What do you mean, my Lord?

HAMLET [*suddenly serious*]: The King and Queen wrote to you, didn't they?

GUILDENSTERN [*looking at the ground*]: Yes, my Lord.

HAMLET: And I can tell you why. During the last few days, I've felt very strange. The world has lost all meaning. Nothing seems beautiful. Men can't please me [*Rosencrantz laughs.*] and women can't either.

ROSENCRANTZ: My Lord, we didn't know.

'Words, words, words.'

HAMLET: So why did you laugh when I said, 'Men can't please me'?

ROSENCRANTZ: Because we passed a group of actors on our way to the castle. They're coming here to act for you. If men can't please you, you won't enjoy their play very much.

HAMLET [*suddenly interested*]: But I like plays. Who are the actors?

[*There is the sound of music outside.*]

GUILDENSTERN: They're arriving now.

HAMLET [*shouting loudly into the air towards the window*]: My good men, welcome to Elsinore! I must politely shake your hands, because you'll see me acting strangely later. My actions will seem funnier than your play. [*quietly to Rosencrantz and Guildenstern*] You see, I've played a joke on my uncle-father and aunt-mother.

GUILDENSTERN: A joke, my Lord?

HAMLET: They think that I'm crazy. But I'm only crazy some of the time. Now, my good friends, I'll see you later tonight. Welcome to Elsinore.

ROSENCRANTZ and GUILDENSTERN: Thank you, my Lord. Goodbye. [*They leave.*]

HAMLET: Now I'm alone, a prisoner of my thoughts. Oh, what a useless man I am! I'm the least brave of men. If I'm so brave, why haven't I taken my revenge? Why haven't I killed my father's murderer and fed his body to the birds? [*wildly*] Oh, my uncle is a wicked man, with my father's blood on his hands! Wicked, heartless man! I must have revenge! [*suddenly calm*] But it's possible that I'm wrong. How can I be sure that it was an honest ghost? In my grief, perhaps I made a mistake. Perhaps it wasn't really the ghost of my father. No, I must be completely sure. I must think of a plan . . . [*thinking*] I've heard that a good play can sometimes show the wicked secrets in a bad man's heart. I'll ask the actors for a story which is similar to the murder of my father. If the Ghost's words are true, the play will make my uncle nervous. Yes, the play's the key to the secrets of his heart. [*He leaves.*]

Act 3   Dark Secrets

Scene 1   The same large room in the castle

[*Claudius, Gertrude, Polonius, Ophelia, Rosencrantz and Guildenstern come in.*]

CLAUDIUS [*to Rosencrantz and Guildenstern*]: So you have no idea why he is so crazy?

ROSENCRANTZ: He says that he feels worried. But he didn't tell us why.

GUILDENSTERN: When we ask him questions, he acts strangely.

GERTRUDE: Did he welcome you warmly?

ROSENCRANTZ: Very politely.

GUILDENSTERN: But it was difficult for him.

GERTRUDE: Did you try to make him happy?

ROSENCRANTZ: Madam, we passed a group of actors on our way here. When we told him about them, he seemed very pleased. They are going to act a play for him tonight.

POLONIUS [*to Claudius and Gertrude*]: That's true. And he asked me to invite you both to see the play.

CLAUDIUS: This is good news. [*to Rosencrantz and Guildenstern*] Go to him and interest him in the play as much as you can.

ROSENCRANTZ: We will, my Lord.

[*Rosencrantz and Guildenstern leave.*]

CLAUDIUS: Sweet Gertrude, leave us too. Polonius and I have sent for Hamlet to come here. He will have an 'accidental' meeting with Ophelia, and we will listen to their conversation from the next room. Then we can judge the real reason for his madness.

GERTRUDE: I shall do what you ask. [*to Ophelia*] I hope that my son's wildness is a result of his love for you. Then, with sweetness and kindness, you can make him well again. [*She leaves through the main doors.*]

POLONIUS [*taking Ophelia to a chair*]: Ophelia, sit here. [*giving her a Bible*] Read this. Hamlet will understand why you're alone. Now I can hear him coming. [*to Claudius*] Let's hide, my Lord.

[*Polonius and Claudius hide behind the small door at the back of the room. Hamlet comes in through the main doors.*]

HAMLET [*to himself*]: To be, or not to be? That's the question. Is it better to suffer bad luck in silence? Or is it better to fight it? Neither of them matter. When we die, we sleep – nothing more. Sleep will end the heartache and the pain of life. It's the best way to end our suffering. To die, to sleep, perhaps to dream – ah, that's the problem. Who knows what terrible dreams wait for us after death? Some of us are unhappy with the pain of life. But we're afraid that the pain of death will be even worse. Death is an undiscovered country. It frightens us. No traveller ever returns. We prefer to suffer the known problems of life than to escape to the unknown problems of death. But it's bad to think too much about this. We become weak, and all our thoughts of action disappear. [*He notices Ophelia.*] But here's my fair Ophelia! Beautiful child, remember me when you speak to God.

OPHELIA: My good Lord, how are you today?

HAMLET [*with great politeness*]: Very well, thank you.

OPHELIA: I have more letters from you. I've wanted to return them to you for a long time. [*holding out the letters*] Please take them.

HAMLET [*shaking his head*]: I never sent you any letters.

OPHELIA [*unable to understand*]: My Lord, you know very well that they're yours. Please take them.

HAMLET: Are you an honest woman?

OPHELIA: I don't understand.

HAMLET: An honest woman must forget that she's pretty. Prettiness can make an honest woman bad, but honesty cannot make a pretty woman good. In the past, I found that hard to believe. Now I know that it's true. I was in love with you.

OPHELIA: I believed you.

HAMLET: You were wrong to believe me. I didn't love you.

OPHELIA [*sadly*]: Then I was wrong.

HAMLET [*softly*]: Give your life to God. You mustn't mix with men or be the mother of their children. Men lie. Believe none of us. Give your life to God and work for the Church. [*He hears a noise behind the small door and looks at Ophelia angrily.*] Where's your father?

OPHELIA: At home, my Lord.

HAMLET [*angrily*]: Lock him in. Then no one will see how stupid he is. Goodbye.

OPHELIA [*lifting her hands to the sky and crying*]: Oh, help him, dear, sweet Heaven!

HAMLET [*angrily*]: Go to a church! Go now! Or if you have to marry, marry a stupid man. Wise men understand too well how women can lie to them. To the church – go now!

OPHELIA: Please, God, make him well!

HAMLET: I've heard about the way that you women paint your faces. God has given you one face, but you paint another face on yourselves. You dance when you walk. You sing when you speak. You want men to believe that you know nothing. I've had enough of it. It's made me crazy. No more talk about marriage. Join a church! [*He leaves through the main doors.*]

OPHELIA: Oh, how can a great man fall so low? A prince, a student, a soldier, the flower of his country, the mirror of everyone's dreams – all gone! He was so brave, clever and beautiful. He was the most perfect of men. He filled my ears

17

with the sweet music of his promises. But now he fills them with the crazy words of a broken mind. Oh, why did this terrible thing have to happen?

[*Claudius and Polonius come in through the small door.*]

CLAUDIUS: Love? I do not think so. His words were a bit wild, but not completely crazy. His sadness sits on something secret in his heart, in the same way that a bird sits on its eggs. I am worried, because there is something dangerous inside those eggs. I must do something quickly before they open. I shall send him immediately to England. The journey and the change of scene will help him. He will soon forget about his problems and return a happy man. What do you think?

POLONIUS: A good idea. But I still believe that love is the reason for his madness. [*to Ophelia*] Are you all right, Ophelia? You don't have to tell us what Lord Hamlet said. We heard it all. [*to Claudius*] My Lord, with your permission, could the Queen talk to her son in private after the play? She can speak to him honestly, and perhaps discover the true reason for his grief. I will hide behind a curtain and listen to their conversation. If she fails to discover the secret of his unhappiness, you can send him to England.

CLAUDIUS: I agree. It is dangerous when important people lose their minds. We must watch them carefully.

[*They leave.*]

Scene 2   Another large room in the castle

[*There is a stage at one end of the room facing empty chairs. Hamlet and Horatio come in from different sides of the stage.*]

HAMLET [*happily*]: Horatio! I'm glad to see you.
HORATIO: My Lord.

HAMLET: I have something to tell you. There's a play tonight in front of the King. I've chosen one with a scene that shows something very similar to my father's death. When the actors are doing that scene, watch my uncle carefully. If the Ghost was honest, the wicked secret in my uncle's heart will show on his face. I'll watch him carefully, too. After the play, we'll compare judgements. But quick! They're coming. I must seem calm. Go to your place.

[*To the sound of music, Claudius, Gertrude, Polonius, Ophelia, Rosencrantz, Guildenstern, and many lords and ladies come in and sit down around the stage.*]

CLAUDIUS: How is everything, dear Hamlet?

HAMLET: The food is good. I am eating the promise-filled air. You cannot feed chickens with that.

CLAUDIUS: I understand nothing of your answer.

HAMLET [*to Rosencrantz*]: Are the actors ready?

ROSENCRANTZ: Yes, my Lord. They are waiting for permission to begin.

GERTRUDE: Come, Hamlet, sit next to me.

HAMLET: No thank you, Mother. I'd prefer to sit here. [*He sits next to Ophelia.*] [*playfully to Ophelia*] Lady, can I lie across your knees?

OPHELIA [*her face going red*]: You are joking, my Lord.

HAMLET: What can a man do in this company if he can't joke? Look at my mother. *She's* happy, and my father's only been dead for two hours.

OPHELIA: He died four months ago.

HAMLET: As long ago as that? So I can put away my black clothes and wear colourful suits again?

[*Music plays. Two actors come onto the stage dressed as a king and queen.*]

FIRST ACTOR [*as the King*]:

> My love, I have to say goodbye
> And sail to foreign lands.
> Don't be sad if I die.
> Marry another man.

SECOND ACTOR [*as the Queen*]:

> A second marriage? Oh, my dear,
> Don't speak to me like this.
> I will never want to feel
> A second husband's kiss!

FIRST ACTOR [*as the King*]:

> But stranger things have happened.
> When a much-loved husband dies,
> A second love soon fills
> A woman's heart and eyes.
> Now I'll sleep here by the flowers.

SECOND ACTOR [*as the Queen*]:

> Death will never kill a love like ours.

[*The 'King' sleeps. The 'Queen' leaves the stage.*]

HAMLET [*to Gertrude*]: How do you like the play?

GERTRUDE: I think that the lady makes too many promises.

HAMLET: Oh, but she'll keep them all.

CLAUDIUS: What is this play about?

HAMLET: It's about the murder of a king in Vienna. It's a frightening story. But honest men like us have nothing to worry about. Only people with wicked secrets in their hearts will feel afraid. [*A third actor comes onto the stage with a small bottle in his hand.*] This is Lucianus, the King's nephew.

THIRD ACTOR [*as Lucianus*]:

> The garden is empty, the bottle is full,
> No one can see, no one can hear.

[*He goes down on his knees next to the 'King'.*]
The palace, the country and Queen will be mine
With one drop of poison in his sleeping ear.
[*He pours the poison into the ear of the 'King'.*]
HAMLET [*to Claudius*]: You'll see now how he wins the love of the dead King's wife.

[*Claudius stands up angrily. His body is shaking and his face is pale.*]

HAMLET [*smiling*]: What? Frightened by a play?
GERTRUDE [*nervously to Claudius*]: What's the matter, my Lord?
POLONIUS [*to the actors*]: Stop the play!
CLAUDIUS: Give me some light. Away from here!
POLONIUS [*shouting*]: Lights! Lights! Lights!

[*Everyone leaves except Hamlet and Horatio.*]

HAMLET [*excitedly*]: Oh, good Horatio, did you see?
HORATIO: I saw everything, my Lord.
HAMLET: So the King doesn't enjoy plays. What a pity! [*loudly*] Come, let's have some music!

[*Rosencrantz and Guildenstern come in.*]

GUILDENSTERN: My Lord, the King . . .
HAMLET [*coldly polite*]: Yes, sir, what's the matter?
GUILDENSTERN: He's in his room and he's sick. The Queen's very worried and has sent me to you.
HAMLET: You're very welcome.
GUILDENSTERN: No, sir. You don't understand. I need a sensible answer.
HAMLET: Sir, I cannot give you a sensible answer because I'm ill in the head. But I'll give you the best answer that I can. What does my mother want?

ROSENCRANTZ: She wants to speak to you in her room before you go to bed.

HAMLET: I will go. [*very coldly*] Do you have any more business with me?

ROSENCRANTZ: Why are you so unfriendly to us? You lock the door on your own happiness if you can't talk freely to your friend.

HAMLET: Sir, I see no future.

ROSENCRANTZ: But you will be the next king of Denmark!

HAMLET: Yes, but while the grass grows, the hungry horse dies. [*An actor comes in carrying some musical pipes.*] Ah, pipes! [*to the actor*] Give one to me. [*He takes a pipe and offers it to Guildenstern.*] Will you play on this for me?

GUILDENSTERN: My Lord, I cannot. I don't know how to play.

HAMLET: It's as easy as lying. Cover these holes with your fingers and thumb, and send air through it from your mouth. You'll hear the most beautiful music.

GUILDENSTERN: But I don't have the skill.

HAMLET [*suddenly angry*]: But you have the skill to play *me*! Make the right moves and you'll discover the secret music of my heart? Am I really easier to play than this pipe? You can try, but you'll never get music from me!

[*Polonius comes in.*]

HAMLET [*suddenly friendly*]: Greetings, sir!

POLONIUS: My Lord, the Queen would like to see you immediately.

HAMLET [*looking through a window at the sky*]: Do you see that cloud? It's shaped like a fish.

POLONIUS [*looking through the window*]: Yes, it *is* like a fish.

HAMLET: I think it's a sheep.

POLONIUS: It has a back like a sheep.

HAMLET: Or like a horse.

POLONIUS: Yes, very like a horse.

HAMLET [*turning away from the window sadly*]: I'll go to my mother soon.

POLONIUS: I will tell her. [*He leaves.*]

HAMLET [*to Rosencrantz and Guildenstern*]: Leave me, friends. [*They leave.*] Now is the darkest time of the night. The ground opens wide and Hell sends its sickness out into the world. I'm thirsty for blood. I'm ready for the business that I have to do. Away, now, to my mother. But I must stay calm. The sharpness of knives will be in my words, not in my hands. [*He leaves.*]

Scene 3   Claudius's room

[*In the room are a large bed, a table and a lot of other expensive furniture. Claudius, Rosencrantz and Guildenstern come in.*]

CLAUDIUS: You will go to England with a secret letter for the King. You will sail tomorrow morning, and take Hamlet with you. He is becoming more and more dangerous. My position as king is not safe while he is here.

GUILDENSTERN: We will do it. A man must protect his king.

CLAUDIUS: Prepare for your journey immediately. We have to end this danger quickly.

ROSENCRANTZ: We will hurry. [*They leave.*]

[*Polonius comes in.*]

POLONIUS: My Lord, he is going to his mother's room. I will listen to them from behind a curtain. Then I will report their conversation to you before you go to bed.

CLAUDIUS: Thank you, my dear Lord. [*Polonius leaves.*] Oh, my crime is wicked. It is the oldest and worst of crimes – a brother's murder. My hand is covered with my brother's blood. Isn't there rain enough in the sweet sky to wash it clean? I want to speak to God, but what can I say? 'Forgive me for my brother's murder'? I can't say that. The murder has given me my dreams, my country and my Queen. With these things, I can buy everything except God's forgiveness. So what can I do? How can I ask for forgiveness if I'm not really sorry? Oh, my position is impossible! Help me, God! My heart's as hard as stone and my knees refuse to touch the ground, but I must try to speak to you. If I succeed, perhaps everything will be all right. [*He goes slowly down on his knees by his bed and puts his hands together.*]

[*The door opens quietly and Hamlet comes in.*]

HAMLET [*quietly to himself, with his hand on his sword*]: I can easily do it now, while he's talking to God. [*He moves quietly towards Claudius, then stops.*] But if I kill him now, he'll go straight to Heaven. I need to think about this. A wicked man murders my father and I, his only son, send this same man to Heaven? No, that's not revenge. It will be better to wait. I'll kill him when he's drunk too much. Or when he's angry, or in bed with my mother. I want this man to go to Hell, not Heaven. I must be patient. [*quietly, looking at Claudius*] Your words to God have saved you now, but you won't live much longer. [*He leaves.*]

CLAUDIUS [*standing up sadly*]: I speak the words, but there is no feeling in them. Empty words will never reach God's ears.

Scene 4   Gertrude's bedroom

[*In the room are a large, beautiful bed, chairs, and a table with a mirror above it. Large, thick curtains are hanging across the window. Gertrude and Polonius come in.*]

POLONIUS: Do not try to be kind to him. You have protected him for too long. Tell him that his jokes must stop. I will say no more – but please, do not be too soft with him.

HAMLET [*from outside the door*]: Mother! Mother!

'If I kill him now, he'll go straight to Heaven.'

GERTRUDE: There he is. I will do what you say. Now you must hide.

[*Polonius hides behind one of the curtains. Gertrude sits down and Hamlet comes in.*]

HAMLET: Now, Mother, what's the matter?

GERTRUDE: Hamlet, your father's very angry with you.

HAMLET: Mother, my father's very angry with *you*.

GERTRUDE: Why are you so rude?

HAMLET: Why are *you* so *wicked*?

GERTRUDE: What's the matter? Have you forgotten who I am?

HAMLET: Of course not! You're the Queen, your husband's brother's wife. And – poor me! – you're my mother.

GERTRUDE [*standing up angrily*]: I can't speak to you when you're like this.

HAMLET: No, sit down. [*He angrily pushes her down into her chair.*] You're not leaving until I've shown you the wickedness of your heart.

GERTRUDE [*frightened*]: What are you going to do? Are you going to murder me? [*shouting*] Help!

POLONIUS [*from behind the curtain*]: Murder? Help!

HAMLET [*taking out his sword and looking at the curtain*]: Ah! The *real* criminal! Revenge at last!

[*He pushes the sword through the curtain and kills Polonius. Polonius falls to the floor with the curtain over his face.*]

GERTRUDE [*putting her hands to her face and crying*]: Oh, no! What have you done?

HAMLET: I don't know. Is it the King?

GERTRUDE [*angrily*]: Oh, what a wicked, stupid act!

HAMLET: Yes, a wicked act. Almost as bad, dear Mother, as marrying your husband's murderer.

GERTRUDE: My husband's murderer?

HAMLET: Yes, that's what I said. [*He goes down on one knee and uncovers Polonius's face.*] [*sadly*] You silly man, what were you doing here? I thought you were the King. [*standing up slowly, looking down at the body*] But your death is *your* mistake. You were listening to other people's conversations. That's a dangerous game. [*turning to Gertrude*] Stop crying and sit down. Save your grief for your real crime. Listen to your heart, if it's not already as hard as stone.

GERTRUDE: What have I done wrong? Why are you so unkind to me?

HAMLET: Your wicked act has made a lie of everything good. It's made the beautiful words of a wedding promise as ugly as the bad language of a drinker. It's taken the heart out of a marriage. It's turned sweet religion into a meaningless list of words. Heaven's face turns away with grief, and the Earth's is red with sickness at your act.

GERTRUDE: What act are you talking about?

HAMLET [*showing her the small picture of his father around his neck*]: Look at this man, standing bravely like a god. This was your husband – a real man! [*showing her the small picture of Claudius around her neck*] Compare that man with this one. Your new husband is like a dying plant, poisoning the memory of his perfect brother with his smell. Can't you see? What judgement has taken you from this [*pointing to the picture of his father*] to this [*pointing to the picture of Claudius*]? What has robbed you of your senses? Oh, crime, where is your punishment? If judgement is as weak as this in a sensible woman's heart, what hope is there of goodness in the world?

GERTRUDE [*crying*]: Oh, Hamlet, that's enough. You've turned my eyes into my own heart. Nothing can wash away the darkness that I see.

HAMLET: But still you sleep in a dirty bed. You make love in sheets that smell of pigs.

GERTRUDE [*holding his arm*]: Stop it, sweet Hamlet! These words are like knives in my ears.

HAMLET [*pushing her away*]: A murderer and a <u>thief</u>. A man who stole the circle of gold from my father's head.

GERTRUDE [*crying*]: Stop!

HAMLET: A king with blood-covered clothes . . . [*The ghost of Hamlet's father comes in and sits down in an empty chair.*] [*looking at the Ghost*] Save me and protect me, you heavenly guards!

GERTRUDE [*to herself, unable to see the Ghost*]: Oh, no. He's really mad.

HAMLET [*to the Ghost*]: Do not be angry with your son. He still remembers his promise to you.

GHOST: Do not forget: be kind to your mother. She does not understand what is happening. Speak softly to her.

HAMLET [*softly to Gertrude*]: How are you feeling, my Lady?

GERTRUDE [*worried*]: How are *you* feeling? Your eyes are wild and your hair's standing up on end. Oh, sweet son, be less angry and more patient. Tell me, what can you see?

HAMLET [*pointing at the Ghost*]: Do you see nothing there?

GERTRUDE: Nothing at all.

HAMLET: Do you *hear* nothing either?

GERTRUDE: No, nothing.

[*The Ghost stands up and starts to leave.*]

HAMLET: Look, it's leaving. My father, in his everyday clothes.

[*The Ghost leaves.*]

GERTRUDE: You're imagining it. Dreams seem real when your mind is sick.

HAMLET: Sick? My mind and body are as healthy as yours. [*holding his mother's hand*] I'm not mad. If you believe that, you're lying to yourself. Don't turn your eyes away from the darkness inside you, or it will eat your heart. If you say sorry for your past mistakes, goodness will return to all our lives.

GERTRUDE: Oh, Hamlet, you've cut my heart in two.

HAMLET: Throw away the bad half, and live with the good, clean half. Don't go to my uncle's bed. He'll soon accept that he must spend his nights without you. I'll kiss you as your son when you've asked God for forgiveness. [*looking at Polonius's body*] And I'll ask God's forgiveness for this. This accident is Heaven's way of punishing me. I'll take him away and think of an excuse for his death. [*looking at Gertrude*] You know I have to go to England?

GERTRUDE: It's decided?

HAMLET: Rosencrantz and Guildenstern are going with me, and they have an unopened letter with the King's secret orders. They're working with the King against me, but I'll discover their secret. Then I'll destroy them all together. [*looking down at Polonius's body*] Now, I'll take this body into the next room. In life, this silly man spoke so many empty words. In death, he looks so quiet and serious. [*taking Polonius by the legs*] Come, sir, our conversations are finished. Goodnight, Mother.

[*Hamlet pulls Polonius away. Gertrude follows him out of the room.*]

Act 4 Wicked Plans

Scene 1 Claudius's room

[*Claudius and Gertrude come in.*]

CLAUDIUS: You look unhappy. How's your son?

GERTRUDE: As mad as a storm at sea. While he was shouting at me, he heard a noise from behind the curtain. Without thinking, he took out his sword. Then he killed good Polonius.

CLAUDIUS [*angrily*]: A terrible crime! But of course, he thought that he was killing *me*. I have been too kind to him. Because I tried to hide his madness, a good man has lost his life. Where is Hamlet now?

GERTRUDE: He is taking away the body. But even in his madness, there is still some good in him. He is very sorry about Polonius's death.

CLAUDIUS: I shall send him away before the sun comes up. [*calling*] Guildenstern! [*Rosencrantz and Guildenstern come in.*] Good friends, Hamlet has killed Polonius and is trying to hide the body. Find him immediately, and take the body into the church. [*Rosencrantz and Guildenstern hurry away.*] Come, Gertrude, we shall call our wisest friends and tell them the terrible news. But we must be careful how we tell them. We don't want any punishment to fall on us. Come quickly!

[*Claudius and Gertrude leave.*]

Scene 2   *The castle stairs*

[*Hamlet comes down the stairs. Rosencrantz and Guildenstern meet him at the bottom.*]

ROSENCRANTZ: What have you done with the body, my Lord?

HAMLET [*coldly*]: How does a king's son reply when he's questioned by a dog?

ROSENCRANTZ: Are you calling me a dog, my Lord?

HAMLET: Yes, because you accept the King's smiles and gifts, and follow all his orders.

ROSENCRANTZ: I don't understand you, my Lord.

HAMLET: Good. Clever words mean nothing to a stupid ear.

ROSENCRANTZ: My Lord, you must tell us where the body is.

HAMLET: You'll have to catch me first!

[*Hamlet runs away. Rosencrantz and Guildenstern hurry after him.*]

Scene 3   Claudius's room

[*Claudius is in the room with two or three servants. Rosencrantz and Guildenstern come in.*]

CLAUDIUS: What news?

ROSENCRANTZ: He will not tell us where the body is.

CLAUDIUS: But where is *he*?

ROSENCRANTZ: He is waiting outside, my Lord, under guard.

CLAUDIUS [*shouting*]: Bring him in! [*Soldiers bring Hamlet in.*] Now, Hamlet, where's Polonius?

HAMLET: At supper.

CLAUDIUS [*angrily*]: At supper? Where?

HAMLET: *He* isn't eating. Worms are eating *him*. Worms have the best food in the world. The fat king with his country and the thin man with no job are just different dishes in the same meal. We all feed worms in the end.

CLAUDIUS [*angrily*]: Where is Polonius?

HAMLET [*smiling coldly*]: In Heaven. Send a messenger to find him. If he isn't there, *you* can look for him in Hell. Or, if you wait for a month, you'll smell him somewhere near the stairs.

CLAUDIUS [*to the soldiers*]: Look for him there. [*The soldiers leave.*] Hamlet, I must send you away immediately. The ship is ready. Your friends are waiting to take you to England.

HAMLET: To England? Good. [*turning away and laughing wildly*] Away to England! [*to Claudius*] Goodbye, dear Mother.

CLAUDIUS [*coldly*]: Your loving *father*, Hamlet.

HAMLET: Father and mother are man and wife. They are one – they are the same. And so, *Mother*, goodbye! [*He leaves.*]

CLAUDIUS [*nervously to Rosencrantz and Guildenstern*]: Follow him on foot. I want him away tonight. Hurry! [*Rosencrantz and Guildenstern leave.*] [*to himself*] Soon I want to hear news of Hamlet's death. Until then I cannot be happy. [*He leaves.*]

Scene 4   The same large room as in act 2 scene 2

[*Gertrude is with Horatio. Ophelia comes in. Her eyes are wild and she is smiling like a madwoman.*]

GERTRUDE: What's the matter, Ophelia?
OPHELIA [*singing*]:

> He is dead and gone, Lady.
> He is dead and gone.
> At his head a piece of grass,
> At his feet, a stone.

GERTRUDE [*softly*]: Oh, Ophelia . . .
OPHELIA [*singing*]: His face as white as mountain snow –

[*Claudius comes in through the small door.*]

GERTRUDE [*quietly to Claudius*]: Listen to this, my Lord.
OPHELIA [*singing*]:

> His body cold as ice.
> There are no flowers on his grave
> Or tears in people's eyes.

CLAUDIUS [*smiling sweetly*]: How are you, my pretty Lady?
OPHELIA: We know what we are. Not what we can become.
CLAUDIUS [*to Gertrude*]: She's talking about her father.
OPHELIA [*singing*]:

> Tomorrow is the day of love.
> The sky is shining blue.
> I'm standing at my window,
> Dreaming, Love, of you.

CLAUDIUS [*very surprised and worried*]: Pretty Ophelia!
OPHELIA [*laughing, dancing and singing wildly*]:

> 'Why will you not marry me?'
> the pretty young girl said.
> 'There's no need,' the boy replied.
> 'You're already in my bed!'

CLAUDIUS [*to Gertrude*]: How long has she been like this?

OPHELIA [*laughing and dancing wildly*]: I can't stop crying when I think of him in the cold ground. My brother will hear of this. So thank you for your kind words. Bring me my horse! Good night, Ladies, goodnight. [*She dances out of the room.*]

CLAUDIUS [*to Horatio*]: Follow her and watch her carefully. [*Horatio leaves.*] This is the poison of deep grief. It all comes from her father's death. Oh, Gertrude, one sadness quickly follows another. First her father is killed, then your son is gone. People are talking because we put Polonius into his grave so quickly and secretly. Now poor Ophelia has lost her mind and her brother has returned from France. This is worse than a thousand deaths.

[*There is a loud noise of shouting and fighting outside.*]

CLAUDIUS [*nervously*]: Where are my guards? They must stand by the door! [*A messenger arrives.*] What's the matter?

MESSENGER: Save yourself, my Lord. An angry crowd has broken through the castle gates and is coming this way. Laertes is with them, and they want him to be king!

[*There is a louder noise of fighting and shouting. The main doors open suddenly and Laertes runs in with his followers.*]

LAERTES [*angrily, sword in hand*]: Where's the King? [*Noticing the King and Queen alone, he turns to his followers.*] Wait outside, all of you. And guard the door. [*His followers leave. Laertes walks towards the King and points his sword at his neck.*] Give me my father!

CLAUDIUS [*proud but nervous*]: Stay calm, good Laertes. Tell me, what is the reason for all this? Why are you so angry?

LAERTES: Where is my father?

CLAUDIUS: Dead.

LAERTES: How did it happen? Don't play games with me. You're the King, but I'm not afraid of you. It doesn't matter what happens to me in this world or the next. But I will have revenge for my father!

CLAUDIUS: Good Laertes, in your revenge for your father's death, will you attack both his friends and enemies?

LAERTES: Only his enemies.

CLAUDIUS [*smiling and pushing the sword away from his neck*]: Now you speak like a good son and an honest man. My heart is filled with grief at your father's death. I did not kill him.

[*The small door opens and Ophelia comes in. Her clothes are dirty, her hair is untidy. She walks slowly around the room, not looking at anyone. She is talking quietly to herself.*]

LAERTES [*realising that his sister is mad*]: Someone's going to pay for this! [*going to Ophelia and speaking softly*] Kind sister, sweet Ophelia! Is it possible for a young girl's mind to die as easily as an old man's body?

OPHELIA [*singing*]: There were no flowers on his grave,
      But tears fell down like rain.
      [*smiling like a child, holding out her hand to Laertes*] Here's a flower for memory, and here's a flower for thought. A flower of sadness for you, and another one for me. I wanted to give you a flower of love. But it died when my father died.

LAERTES: Her meaningless words shine like stars in the darkness of Hell.

OPHELIA [*dancing away and singing*]:
      Will he not come back again?
      No, no, he will never come again. [*She leaves.*]

LAERTES [*shouting to Claudius*]: Did you see that? Oh, God!

CLAUDIUS [*calmly*]: Laertes, I understand your grief, but I am not your father's murderer. If you can prove me wrong, I will give you everything, even my life.

34

'Someone's going to pay for this!'

LAERTES: If you are not his murderer, who *is*? Why was his death so secret? Why are there no flowers on his grave? I will not rest until I have found the answer to these questions.

CLAUDIUS: And I will help you to find them. Then you will have my permission to bring your sword down on his murderer's head. Please, come with me.

[*They leave.*]

Scene 5   Inside the castle gates

[*It is a cold, grey afternoon. Horatio is dressed warmly, walking in the snow. A sailor comes in.*]

SAILOR: I have a letter for you, sir. It is from a man who was sailing to England. If your name is Horatio, it is for you.

HORATIO [*taking the letter and reading*]: *Horatio, robbers attacked us at sea two days out of Denmark. During the fight, I climbed onto the robbers' ship and became their prisoner. They freed me in return for my promise of help. This man has letters for the King. After he has given them to him, he will bring you to me. Hurry! I have news for you that you will not believe. Hamlet.* [*to the sailor*] Take your letters to the King. Then take me immediately to the man who gave them to you.

[*They leave.*]

Scene 6   Claudius's room

[*Claudius and Laertes are sitting at the table.*]

CLAUDIUS: You have listened intelligently to the facts. Now you must think of me as your friend. Your father's murderer really wanted to kill *me*.

LAERTES: But why haven't you punished him?

CLAUDIUS: For two reasons. First, the Queen, his mother, loves

36

him very much. She is important to me, and I do not want to hurt her. Second, he is very popular with the ordinary people in this country. He can do nothing wrong in their eyes, so I cannot openly punish him.

LAERTES: Death has taken my dear, good father, and madness has taken my perfect sister. But my revenge will come.

CLAUDIUS: Do not worry about that. I have made plans, and you will soon hear more. I loved your father as I love myself. [*A messenger arrives with letters.*] But what news is this?

MESSENGER: Letters, my Lord, from Hamlet. These are for you, and this one is for the Queen.

CLAUDIUS [*angry and surprised*]: From Hamlet? Who brought them?

MESSENGER: A sailor, my Lord, but I did not see him.

CLAUDIUS [*taking the letters*]: Laertes, you can hear them. [*to the messenger*] Leave us. [*The messenger leaves. Claudius reads the first letter.*] *I am coming back to Denmark. Very soon, I shall request permission to speak to you. Then I shall explain the reasons for my sudden and even stranger return. Hamlet.* [*looking nervously at Laertes*] What does this mean?

LAERTES: I do not know. But I am glad he has returned. I want to call him 'murderer' to his face.

CLAUDIUS: I have an idea that will give you your revenge. We can punish him in a way that will look like an accident. Even his mother will not know what we have planned.

LAERTES [*interested*]: I want to be the one who punishes him.

CLAUDIUS: Perfect! While you were away in France, reports reached this country of your wonderful sword-fighting skills. When Hamlet heard these reports, he felt angry. He hoped for your sudden return. He wanted to test *his* skill with a sword against yours. Now Hamlet is going to return. What would you most like to do to him?

LAERTES [*angrily*]: Cut his neck open in the church!

CLAUDIUS: No place, not even a church, can protect a murderer from his punishment. But, good Laertes, listen to me. Stay away from Hamlet when he first arrives. I will send people to talk to him about your skill with the sword. He will become excited and want to fight you. Before the fight, you can secretly take the protector off your sword. Then you can take revenge on him for the death of your father.

LAERTES: I will do it. And I have some poison that I can put on the end of my sword. I only have to touch him with it and he will die.

CLAUDIUS: If our plan fails, I have another idea. He will become hot and thirsty during a long, hard fight. I will put some poison in a drink and offer it to him. [*The door opens.*] Quiet! What is that noise. [*Gertrude comes in, looking pale. Claudius stands up.*] What is it, my sweet Queen?

GERTRUDE: Oh, there's too much sadness. Your sister is dead, Laertes.

LAERTES [*standing up and shaking*]: Dead? Where?

GERTRUDE: She was sitting in a tree by a stream, making circles of dead flowers for her hair. Suddenly, she fell. She lay on her back in the icy water, singing to herself. Then, slowly, the weight of the water in her clothes pulled her down – and she died.

LAERTES [*quietly to Claudius*]: Goodbye, my Lord. I have words of fire to speak. But first I have a thousand tears to cry. [*He leaves.*]

CLAUDIUS: Let's follow him, Gertrude. I calmed him, but this will make him angry again. I don't want him to do anything silly.

[*They leave.*]

Act 5   Final Acts of Revenge

Scene 1   A snowy field of graves at night, with trees all around

[*A man is singing and working in a grave. Hamlet and Horatio watch the man quietly from the trees for a minute. Then Hamlet walks towards the man.*]

HAMLET: How long have you worked here?

WORKMAN: For thirty years. I started on the same day that young Hamlet was born. The mad prince – the one they sent to England.

HAMLET [*interested*]: And why was he sent to England?

WORKMAN: Because they're all as mad as he is over there.

HAMLET [*going down on one knee next to the grave*]: How long will a man lie in the earth before the worms eat him?

WORKMAN: Some people last longer than others. [*He gives Hamlet a skull.*] This one, for example, has been here for twenty-three years.

HAMLET: Whose was it?

WORKMAN: It belonged to Yorick, the King's joker.

HAMLET [*quietly*]: Can I see it? [*He takes the skull and looks into its empty eyes.*] Poor Yorick. I knew him – a very funny man. He carried me on his back a thousand times. Now where is the face that I kissed so often? Where are the jokes that everybody laughed at? Show yourself to my Lady, the Queen, now. It doesn't matter how brightly she colours her face. In the end, she will look the same as you. [*There are noises, coming closer. Hamlet looks up.*] But quiet. Someone's coming. [*Claudius, Gertrude, Laertes, a churchman and some lords arrive with the body of Ophelia. Hamlet returns the skull to the ground, stands up and moves quickly back to the trees.*] [*quietly to Horatio*] Here come the King and Queen. Who are they carrying so quietly to the grave? Let's hide in the shadows and watch.

LAERTES: Put her in the earth, so flowers can grow from her beautiful young body.

HAMLET [*quietly to Horatio*]: What! The fair Ophelia?

[*Ophelia's body is lowered carefully into her grave.*]

GERTRUDE: Sweet Lady, goodbye. [*She drops flowers into the grave.*] I wanted to put flowers on your wedding bed, not your grave.

LAERTES [*wild with grief*]: Death to the man whose wicked act took away your mind! Hold back the earth until I have kissed her one last time. [*He jumps into the grave and kisses Ophelia.*] Now build a mountain of earth above her that will touch the sky.

HAMLET [*walking out of the trees*]: Who is this whose grief brings pity even to the eyes of Heaven?

LAERTES [*climbing out of the grave and running at Hamlet*]: I'll send you to Hell! [*He puts his hands around Hamlet's neck.*]

HAMLET [*angrily defending himself*]: Take your hands off me!

CLAUDIUS [*pulling Laertes away*]: Stop!

GERTRUDE [*pulling Hamlet away*]: Hamlet! Hamlet!

HORATIO [*holding Hamlet's arm*]: My Lord, calm down.

HAMLET [*shouting angrily*]: I loved Ophelia too! Forty thousand brothers could not love her as much as I did!

CLAUDIUS [*holding Laertes by the arm*]: He is crazy, Laertes.

GERTRUDE [*to Laertes*]: For the love of God, do not fight him. This is madness, but it will soon pass.

HAMLET [*to Laertes*]: You are unfair to me, sir. If you act like a dog, I can act like one, too!

CLAUDIUS [*to Horatio*]: Please, Horatio, take him away. [*Hamlet and Horatio leave. Claudius turns and speaks quietly to Laertes.*] Remember our conversation last night. Be patient. [*to everyone*] Do not worry. We shall all soon be safe from danger.

[*They leave.*]

Scene 2 *The same large room as in act 1 scene 1*

[*Hamlet and Horatio come in.*]

HAMLET: One night on the ship, I went to Rosencrantz and Guildenstern's room. [*holding up a letter*] I found this letter from the King and brought it back to my room. In it, he gave orders for my death!

HORATIO [*unable to believe it*]: Is it possible?

HAMLET [*giving him the letter*]: You can read it. But before you do, hear the rest of my story. With enemies all around me, I had to act fast. I wrote another letter in the King's handwriting and returned it to Rosencrantz and Guildenstern's room. In it, I asked the King of England to put the messengers to sudden death. The next day, we were attacked by robbers. You know how the story ends.

HORATIO: So Rosencrantz and Guildenstern went to their death?

HAMLET: I don't feel bad about it. They were destroyed by their own dishonesty.

HORATIO [*angrily*]: What kind of king is your uncle?

HAMLET: He killed my father and sleeps with my mother. He's destroyed my happiness and has tried to take my life. Now he has to pay for his crimes.

HORATIO: There isn't much time. He'll soon hear the news from England.

HAMLET: I don't need much time. A man's life is no more than one touch with a sword. But I'm very sorry about Laertes. His grief is similar to mine. I'll try to be friends with him again.

[*Osric comes in and takes off his hat.*]

OSRIC [*to Hamlet*]: My Lord, I have a message for you from the King. Laertes has just arrived at court. He is a perfect man. Everybody likes him, and he is excellent with the sword.

HAMLET: You describe him very well. But what's the reason for your wonderful description of him?

OSRIC: The King invites you to a friendly swordfight with Laertes. Will you accept the invitation?

HAMLET: And if I say no?

OSRIC [*surprised*]: My Lord, what will people think if you refuse?

HAMLET [*smiling*]: This is a good time of day for exercise. Tell the King that I'm ready.

OSRIC: I am your servant, my Lord. [*He leaves.*]

HORATIO [*worried*]: You'll lose this fight, my Lord.

HAMLET: I don't think so. While Laertes was in France, I did a lot of practice. [*quietly*] But I have a bad feeling in my heart about all this.

HORATIO: If your heart isn't happy, listen to it. I'll tell the King that you're not well.

HAMLET [*proudly*]: Impossible! I refuse to listen to the voice of fear.

[*Music plays. Servants come in and prepare a table with cups of wine. Officers come in carrying swords and knives. Claudius, Gertrude, Laertes, Osric and other lords, officers and servants come in.*]

HAMLET [*walking towards Laertes and shaking his hand*]: I'm sorry, sir, for the bad things that I've done. But believe me, they were not planned. It was the illness in my mind that did these things. It was not me. I'm not your enemy, but this madness is mine. So please, sir, forgive Hamlet for his crimes.

LAERTES [*seriously*]: As a man, I forgive you. But as a son and a brother, I can't. I must defend the good name of my family.

HAMLET: I understand. Now I'll gladly test your skill with the sword. [*to Osric*] Give us the swords. Hurry!

[*Osric takes a number of swords from the officers. Hamlet and Laertes choose their swords and prepare to fight.*]

CLAUDIUS [*loudly*]: Begin.

[*Hamlet and Laertes fight. Hamlet touches Laertes with his sword.*]

HAMLET: One hit!

LAERTES: No!

HAMLET [*to Osric*]: Your judgement?

OSRIC: A hit – a very clear hit.

LAERTES [*pointing his sword at Hamlet*]: Again.

CLAUDIUS: One minute! Give me a cup of wine. [*A servant gives him a cup. Claudius secretly puts poison in the cup, then holds it up.*] Hamlet, here's to your health. [*to a servant*] Give him the cup.

HAMLET: I'll drink it later. [*to Laertes*] Come. [*They fight again. Hamlet touches Laertes with his sword.*] Another hit! What do you say?

LAERTES: He touched me, I agree.

CLAUDIUS [*to Gertrude*]: Our son will win.

GERTRUDE [*taking the cup from Claudius and smiling at Hamlet*]: The Queen drinks to your good luck, Hamlet. [*She lifts the cup to her mouth.*]

CLAUDIUS [*nervously*]: Gertrude, don't drink.

GERTRUDE: I will, my Lord. Forgive me. [*She drinks, and walks towards Hamlet with the cup.*]

CLAUDIUS [*quietly to himself*]: It is the poisoned cup. It is too late.

HAMLET [*to Gertrude*]: Not yet. I'll drink it later.

GERTRUDE [*taking a white cloth from her belt*]: Then I shall dry your face.

LAERTES [*secretly putting poison on his sword and turning quietly to Claudius*]: My Lord, I'll hit him now. But my heart tells me that this is wrong.

HAMLET [*pointing his sword at Laertes*]: Let's fight for the third time, Laertes. This time, do your best. [*rudely*] You're fighting like a child.

LAERTES [*pointing his sword angrily at Hamlet*]: Is that what you think? Let's see!

[*They fight angrily for a long time. Finally, Laertes cuts Hamlet with his sword. They continue fighting. Laertes drops his sword. Hamlet throws his sword to Laertes and picks up Laertes's sword. The fight continues and Hamlet cuts Laertes. Suddenly, Gertrude falls to the floor.*]

HAMLET [*running to Gertrude*]: How's the Queen?

CLAUDIUS [*nervously*]: The excitement has made her ill.

GERTRUDE [*to Hamlet*]: No, no, the drink, the drink! Oh, my dear Hamlet, I am poisoned! [*She dies.*]

HAMLET [*shouting angrily*]: Oh, wicked crime! Lock the doors. Find the murderer!

LAERTES [*pointing weakly to the sword in Hamlet's hand*]: It's here, Hamlet. Hamlet, you're dead. No medicine in the world can save you. [*He falls to the floor.*] You have less than half an hour to live. There's poison on the sword in your hand, and with it you've also killed me. Look, here I lie, and will never get up again. Your mother's poisoned, too. The King's the murderer.

HAMLET [*looking at the sword in his hand*]: The sword is poisoned? Then, poison, do your work. [*He runs at Claudius and pushes the sword into him.*]

EVERYBODY: Murder! Murder!

CLAUDIUS [*in pain*]: You can still defend me, friends. I am only hurt.

HAMLET [*pushing the cup of poisoned wine to Claudius's mouth*]: Here, you wicked, murdering Dane. Drink this wine! [*Claudius drinks.*] Follow my mother! [*Claudius dies.*]

LAERTES: The punishment is good. He's killed by his own poison. [*weakly holding out his hand to Hamlet*] Hamlet, forgive me. You're not my father's murderer or mine. And I'm not yours.

'I am poisoned!'

[*Hamlet takes Laertes's hand. Laertes dies.*]

HAMLET [*to Laertes*]: I'll follow you to Heaven soon. [*He falls to the floor and turns to Horatio.*] I'm dead, Horatio. But you still live.

HORATIO [*lifting the cup of poisoned wine to his mouth*]: I'm not afraid of death. There's still some wine in this cup.

HAMLET [*angrily but weakly*]: Give *me* the cup. Drop it. If you love me, Horatio, don't go to Heaven yet. Stay in this heartless world long enough to tell my story. [*Shouts come from outside.*] What warlike noise is that?

OSRIC: Young Fortinbras won his war in Poland and has returned. [*looking out of the window*] He is welcoming the messenger from the King of England.

HAMLET [*weakly*]: Oh, I'm dying, Horatio! The poison is too strong. I can't live to hear the news from England. But I believe that Fortinbras will make an excellent king of Denmark. Tell him the reasons for all this. The rest is silence. [*He dies.*]

HORATIO: A brave heart has broken. Goodnight, sweet Prince.

[*The doors open. Fortinbras, his soldiers and the King of England's messenger come in.*]

FORTINBRAS [*looking at the four dead bodies*]: What has happened? Oh, proud Death, why have you taken so many princes at the same time to their graves?

MESSENGER: I have come from England too late with our news. The King's request was answered – Rosencrantz and Guildenstern are dead. But who will thank us now?

HORATIO [*looking at Claudius's body*]: Not him. He never gave the orders for their death. [*to Fortinbras*] But now you are here from your Polish wars, I will tell you a sad story of broken dreams, wicked murder and accidental death. This is how it ends. [*pointing to Hamlet, Laertes, Claudius and Gertrude*]

FORTINBRAS: Four officers will carry Hamlet's body away. This country has lost a great man and a wonderful future king. Soldiers' music will play for him as he travels to the next world. [*to his officers*] Take away the bodies. This room looks like a field of war. Go, tell the soldiers to shoot their guns.

[*Everybody leaves. Officers carry the bodies away. There is a short silence, and then the sound of big guns comes from the castle walls.*]

ACTIVITIES

Act 1

Before you read

1 *Hamlet* is one of Shakespeare's most famous plays. Work with another student.
   a What other Shakespeare plays do you know? Make a list.
   b What are those plays about? Are they amusing or sad? Write one or two sentences about each play.
   c Compare your list with the lists of other students. Add plays that are not on your list.

2 Look at the Word List at the back of the book.
   a Which words describe:
      ● people?
      ● parts of a play?
      ● things that are found in the ground?
      ● things that can kill?
   b Choose two other words from the list and use them in sentences.

3 Read the Introduction to the play and answer these questions.
   a In which country do the people in the play live?
   b Who is Hamlet's main enemy?
   c Which of these words does not describe Hamlet?
      honest   ordinary   perfect   thoughtful   brave
   d Which of these words does not describe the play?
      sad   famous   serious   simple   special
   e When did the real Hamlet live?
   f How many plays did Shakespeare write before he wrote *Hamlet*?
   g When was *Hamlet* written?

4 Act 1 is called 'The Ghost on the Castle Wall'. The Ghost is the ghost of Hamlet's father. How do you think Hamlet will feel when he sees the ghost? What will he do?

While you read

5 Who are these people? Draw a line to one of the descriptions on the right.

   a Claudius   Hamlet's friend
   b Fortinbras   Laertes's sister
   c Polonius   Hamlet's mother
   d Laertes   Hamlet's uncle
   e Gertrude   the King of Norway's nephew
   f Horatio   the King of Denmark's friend
   g Ophelia   Polonius's son

After you read

6 Choose the correct answer.

   a The King of Norway
      ● wants to attack Denmark.
      ● lost land to Hamlet's father.
      ● disagrees with his nephew's plans.
   b Hamlet thinks that his mother
      ● did not really love his father.
      ● does not really love him.
      ● knows about the murder of his father.
   c Polonius
      ● wants his son to go to France.
      ● wants his daughter to become the next queen.
      ● does not want his daughter to get into trouble.
   d The Ghost wants Hamlet to
      ● punish the King.
      ● punish the Queen.
      ● punish the King and the Queen.

7 Work with another student. Discuss these questions. What do you think?

   a Does Claudius really love Gertrude?
   b Why did Gertrude agree to marry Claudius?
   c Is Hamlet right to feel angry with his mother?
   d Why does Claudius really want Hamlet to stay in Denmark?

Act 2

Before you read

8 Discuss these questions with another student. What do you think?

   a Will Hamlet take his revenge immediately? Why (not)?

   b What will happen between Hamlet and Ophelia? Why?

While you read

9 Put these in the order they happen. Number them 1–6.

   a Hamlet meets his old friends.   .....

   b Actors arrive at the castle.   .....

   c Ophelia is worried about Hamlet.   .....

   d Hamlet talks to Polonius.   .....

   e There is good news from Norway.   .....

   f Hamlet thinks of a plan.   .....

After you read

10 Are these sentences right or wrong? Correct the ones that are wrong.

   a Hamlet has gone mad because Ophelia refuses to see him.

   b Claudius plans a meeting between Hamlet and Ophelia.

   c Claudius invites Rosencrantz and Guildenstern to the castle.

   d Ophelia has given all Hamlet's letters to her father.

   e Claudius and Gertrude believe that Polonius is right about Hamlet's madness.

   f Hamlet tells Rosencrantz and Guildenstern that he is bored with life.

   g Hamlet tells his friends about the Ghost.

   h Hamlet is sure that his uncle is a murderer.

   i Hamlet is going to choose a play for the actors.

11 Discuss these questions with another student. What do you think?

   a How do these people *really* feel about Hamlet?

      Polonius   Ophelia   Rosencrantz and Guildenstern

      Gertrude   Claudius

   b Why hasn't Hamlet taken revenge on Claudius yet?

Act 3

Before you read

12 Discuss these questions with another student.

    a What is Hamlet's plan? How dangerous is it? Will it work?

    b What will happen when Hamlet meets Ophelia again?

While you read

13 Circle the correct word.

    a Hamlet decides that it is better to *live / die*.

    b Hamlet tells Ophelia to marry a *clever / stupid* man.

    c Claudius *believes / does not believe* that Hamlet is mad.

    d Claudius is *afraid of / angry with* Hamlet.

    e Hamlet is *honest / dishonest* with Horatio.

    f Rosencrantz and Guldenstern *are / are not* spying on Hamlet.

    g Claudius *feels / does not feel* proud of himself.

    h Gertrude *knows / does not know* Claudius's secret.

    i Gertrude *can / cannot* see the Ghost.

    j Hamlet thinks that *Claudius / Polonius* is behind the curtain.

After you read

14 Work with another student. Imagine that you are Gertrude and Claudius. Have this conversation.

    Student A: You are Claudius. You want to send Hamlet away. Explain why.

    Student B: You are Gertrude. You want Hamlet to stay. Explain why.

15 Put these words in the correct places in the sentences below. Use each word only once.

    after   because   before   but   during   if   so
    until   when   while

    a Hamlet is happy … he hears about the actors.

    b '… you have to marry, marry a stupid man,' Hamlet says.

    c Claudius thinks that Hamlet is wild, … not mad.

    d Ophelia's face turns red, … Hamlet jokes with her.

    e Claudius stands up … the play.

    f Hamlet is ill, … he cannot give Guildenstern a sensible answer.

    g Hamlet feels ready for revenge … the play.

  h Claudius doesn't feel safe … Hamlet is still in the country.

  i Polonius will report Hamlet's conversation with Gertrude …
   Claudius goes to bed.

  j Hamlet waits for revenge … Claudius finishes talking to God.

16 Discuss these questions with another student.

  a How does Hamlet feel about these people at the end of Act 3?

   Claudius Rosencrantz and Guildenstern Ophelia

   Polonius Gertrude

  b How do they feel about Hamlet?

  c Who do you feel most sorry for? Why?

Act 4

Before you read

17 Discuss these questions with another student. What problems will
there be if these people meet? Why?

  a Hamlet and Claudius?

  b Hamlet and Ophelia?

  c Claudius and Laertes?

  d Hamlet and Laertes?

While you read

18 Who is speaking? Who or what are they talking about?

  a '*He* isn't eating. Worms are eating
   him.'   …………… ……………

  b 'At his head a piece of grass, at his
   feet, a stone.'   …………… ……………

  c 'This is worse than a thousand deaths.' …………… ……………

  d 'Her meaningless words shine like
   stars.'   …………… ……………

  e 'They freed me in return for my
   promise of help.'   …………… ……………

  f 'I cannot openly punish him.'   …………… ……………

  g 'I want to be the one who punishes
   him.'   …………… ……………

  h 'She lay on her back in the icy water.' …………… ……………

After you read

19 One word in each sentence is wrong. Which word is it? What is the correct word?

  a Hamlet calls Rosencrantz a worm.

  b Ophelia has gone mad because her brother is dead.

  c An angry crowd wants Hamlet to be king.

  d Claudius puts flowers on Polonius's grave.

  e Robbers freed Hamlet in return for his promise of money.

  f Claudius has not punished Hamlet for three reasons.

  g Laertes is sad that Hamlet has returned.

  h Hamlet wants to test Laertes's skill with a gun.

  i Claudius plans to put poison in Hamlet's food.

  j Ophelia jumped out of a tree into an icy stream.

20 Put these words into the correct sentences.

  afraid   fat   kind   mad   patient   safe   secret
  stupid   thin   thirsty   unbelievable

  a Gertrude thinks that Hamlet is ... .

  b Claudius thinks that he has been too ... to Hamlet.

  c Polonius is put into a ... grave.

  d Hamlet thinks that Rosencrantz is ... .

  e 'The ... king with his country and the ... man with no job are just different dishes in the same meal.'

  f Claudius does not feel ... with Hamlet in the country.

  g Laertes does not feel ... of Claudius.

  h Hamlet has ... news for Horatio.

  i Claudius wants Laertes to be ... when Hamlet arrives.

  j If the fight is long, Hamlet will feel ... .

21 Work with another student. Take the parts of Hamlet and the Ghost. Have this conversation.

  Student A: You are the Ghost. Ask Hamlet why he hasn't taken revenge yet. Tell him why he mustn't sail to England.

  Student B: You are Hamlet. Explain why you are going to sail to England. Why are you waiting before you take revenge? Tell the Ghost.

Act 5

Before you read

22 Work with another student. Discuss a possible *happy* ending for this story. How can it happen?

While you read

23 Who

    a is thirty years old? ....

    b died twenty-three years ago? ....

    c puts flowers on Ophelia's grave? ....

    d sent Rosencrantz and Guildenstern to their death? ....

    e brings Hamlet a message from the King? ....

    f doesn't want Hamlet to fight? ....

    g kills Gertrude? ....

    h kills Hamlet? ....

    i does not die? ....

    j does Hamlet want to be the next king of Denmark? ....

After you read

24 Work in small groups. Imagine that you are judges, and discuss these deaths.

Hamlet   Hamlet's father   Gertrude   Claudius
Rosencrantz and Guildenstern   Polonius   Laertes
Ophelia

    a In which order did these people die?

    b Where were they when they died?

    c How did they die?

    d Which deaths were murder? Who was the murderer?

    e Is there anybody alive at the end of the play who should go to prison?

25 Discuss these questions.

    a Why does Laertes forgive Hamlet at the end?

    b Why does Hamlet finally decide to take his revenge? Why didn't he do it earlier?

    c What were Hamlet's biggest mistakes? Why?

Writing

26 Imagine that you are Hamlet. You are studying away from home, in Wittenberg. Write a love letter to Ophelia.

27 Imagine that you are Gertrude. Write a letter to Hamlet in Wittenberg, before this story begins. Explain why you have married Claudius. Ask him to accept Claudius as his new father.

28 You are Claudius. Write your letter to the King of England. Explain why you want him to kill Hamlet.

29 Imagine that you are Rosencrantz or Guildenstern. Write a letter to Hamlet from England, before your death, explaining your actions. Tell him why he should forgive you.

30 Write a report of the death of the King and Queen of Denmark, Hamlet and Laertes for your local newspaper.

31 Write about Hamlet after his death, for a magazine. In what ways was he a good man? What were his weaknesses? What can we learn from his story?

32 Except for Hamlet, who is your favourite person in the play? Who is your least favourite person? Why? Compare them.

33 Imagine that you are Fortinbras. Write a speech to the Danish people, agreeing to become their king. Explain what has happened. Tell them why their future will be better.

34 Imagine that you are going to make a film of the play in your own language. Who will you invite to play the main characters? Where will you film it? Explain why.

35 A student magazine has asked readers to write a modern short story about revenge. The best one will be in the magazine. Write your story.

WORD LIST

act (n) one of the main parts of a play

castle (n) a large, strong building that protected people inside from attack

curtain (n) a piece of hanging cloth that is pulled across a window

ghost (n) a frightening, moving thing in the shape of a person who has died

grave (n) the place in the ground where a dead body is put

grief (n) great sadness, usually after someone has died

God (n) the one who made Heaven and Earth

Heaven (n) the place where good people go after death

Hell (n) the place where bad people go after death

lord (n) a man with a high position because of the family that he comes from

mad (adj) ill in the head

nephew (n) your brother's or sister's son

poison (n/v) something that can kill people or animals. For example, there are poisons in some plants and in the bites of some animals.

revenge (n) your punishment for someone who has hurt you

scene (n) a short part of a play without any change of time or place

servant (n) someone who works in another person's house

skull (n) the hard inside part of the head which gives it its shape

sword (n) a long, sharp piece of metal like a big knife, used for fighting

wicked (adj) very bad and dangerous

worm (n) an animal that lives in the ground, with a long, soft body and no legs